The Buses of Arran, Argyll and environs
in colour photographs by John Sinclair
John Sinclair

Parked in front of *Glen Sannox* displaying its lion emblem on its funnel, a feature first introduced on the ships of The Caledonian Steam Packet Company the previous year, are two Duple bodied Bedford OBs in the fleet of Lennox Transport, based at The Pier Garage, Whiting Bay. This company had been formed in July 1964 from the original company AC Lennox & Sons founded in 1919, with Lennox Motors of Brodick as its subsidiary. This latter company in turn was formed in December 1950 to take over the business of Finlay Kerr-Newton of Brodick operating from the Pier Garage at Brodick, which had only three buses licensed by 1965 as compared with ten in the parent company. SJ1340 had entered service with Gordon Brothers of Lamlash in January 1951, wearing their their striking livery of dark blue, red and light blue with a gold stripe. It competed with AC Lennox on the Brodick to Whiting Bay corridor until the services were coordinated in 1954, and passed with the Gordon business to its rival in February 1961. It was the last new bus delivered to Arran until 1973 when Bedford YRQ CSL400L entered the fleet of Arran Transport and Trading Company, the successor to Lennox Transport. After twenty years running on the island SJ1340 was delicensed, and entered a complex period of preservation which continues to this day. This has involved a return to Brodick in 1993 and a period at The Scottish Vintage Bus Museum at Lathalmond. Parked beside it is identical SJ1243, new in January 1949 to AC Lennox which remained with the company until also withdrawn after twenty years in service.

© John Sinclair, 2018
First published in the United Kingdom, 2018,
by Stenlake Publishing Ltd.
54-58 Mill Square, Catrine, KA5 6RD
www.stenlake.co.uk
ISBN 978-1-84033-834-8

The publishers regret that they cannot supply
copies of any pictures featured in this book.

Printed by
P2D, 1 Newlands Road Westoning, MK45 5LD

Awaiting at Lochranza Pier on 26th July 1965 for the arrival of passengers off the *Duchess of Hamilton* on its thrice weekly, four and a quarter hour long cruise from Gourock to Campbeltown is a selection of buses from all the operators on the island, a scene which was soon to disappear. Entering service in 1932, celebrated for its high-class accommodation with an observation lounge and elegant dining facilities, the excursion steamer was popular for cruises on the Clyde. However, these were in decline by the sixties, and finally ceased at the end of the 1971 summer season. The pier, which had opened in 1888, was then replaced by a slipway for the new car ferry service to Claonaig which started in December 1971. The pier itself was later rebuilt and reopened in 2003 to cater for cruise ships and the paddle steamer *Waverley*. Leading the convoy of coaches is SJ1189 a Commer Commando in the Ribbeck fleet, followed by Lennox Transport's SJ1340 and Leyland Comet DAG64 with a Brockhouse body which had been completed in the Mary Street body shop of Young's Bus Service in Johnstone and the vehicle delivered to Hugh Frazer of Fairlie, a member of Clyde Coast Services. On the other side of the road is DBN627, another Bedford OB, this time in the fleet of Weir of Machrie, which was withdrawn three months later.

Introduction

1965 was another memorable year for me. For the past five years I had been hitch hiking around Scotland, Ireland and Northern England taking colour slides with a 35 mm camera, but this was coming to an end. With over 1300 hits, some overseas, and staying in youth hostels, I had developed a technique which allowed me to travel confidently around the country from location to location. I had built up a slide collection with my main interest being major bus companies such as the Scottish Bus Group and MacBrayne's, and rural bus operation especially in the Highlands and Islands. I was due to graduate in July and start work as a junior doctor, with very little prospect of leisure time in the days of 100 hour working weeks. I therefore turned my attention to areas which, living in Edinburgh, I had neglected. Argyll, Kintyre and the Clyde Coast beckoned. This was fortunate as the sixties proved to be a momentous decade for Scottish operators, and fortuitous for me as I was later to run outreach consultant clinics in Kintyre for 30 years which necessitated overnight stays. Little did I realise that a remote family company with a dozen buses was to become the major national operator it is today and how the name "West Coast Motors" would come to dominate much of the transport scene in Scotland.

By the end of the decade, the vast MacBrayne's empire was being dismantled, and many rural operators were to disappear. Of the eight companies on Arran, five names were still represented in 1965, but three had disappeared within two years. Double deckers were to disappear from Bute within six years. The two dominant companies in Kintyre became one in February 1970, and two smaller operators had disappeared. A hovercraft briefly appeared on the Clyde Coast, and one of the four members of Clyde Coast Services sold out in 1966 and another in 1971. There were also many interesting and unusual buses still on the road including Scottish built Albion chassis, and vehicles with bodies constructed in Scotland. In this book there are photographs of nine vehicles built by Scottish Aviation of Prestwick, three by Brockhouse of Clydebank, one by Croft of Glasgow, one by SCWS, one by McLennan of Spittalfield and two rebuilt by Bennett of Glasgow. There are also pictures of six buses with mail compartments, an additional feature soon to disappear, even on buses in remote areas. Five buses were unique, two were prototypes and three were demonstrators at the Scottish Motor Show.

This colourful scene was not to continue much longer, and this book was written to record the variety of vehicles and liveries to be seen in an area of Scotland very popular with the many who holidayed here at that time, and those who enjoyed a day out in the country or by the seaside. As a reminder of a time, now just a distant memory, nine of the vehicles in this book have been preserved.

Charles Weir had originally started services from Machrie to Lochranza and Brodick with horse-drawn vehicles, introducing motor buses to Brodick Pier in the 1920s. With routes from there to Lenimore and Lochranza to Blackwaterfoot to provide ferry connections, and tours from Machrie and Lenimore, the business continued until 1948 when joint operation of the section between Lochranza Pier and Blackwaterfoot with Donald Robertson of Blackwaterfoot was agreed. He took over the entire operation in May 1951, but this passed back to Weir in 1958 when McMillan handed over the service. This finally passed to Bannatyne Motors on 13th June 1966 with the remainder of Weir's operation which also included a church run from Machrie to Shiskine. The garage was at Machrie, and exchanging passengers on 27th July 1965 are CSS857, an 11 seater Morris J2BM new in 1958 to Turnbull of Gifford and CSD178, a Commer Q4 which had the chassis of a wartime goods vehicle, rebuilt and rebodied by Scottish Aviation in 1949 for Bingham of Girvan, and acquired by Weir in 1961.

Scottish Aviation Limited, based in Prestwick, started manufacturing small aircraft in 1939, but cancellation of Ministry of Aircraft production after the Second World war forced the company to diversify, with the development of a light alloy bus body fitted to a variety of vehicles from 1948 to 1952. Many were on Commer Commando and Albion Victor chassis, but there were four AEC Regal 111s, two for Northern Roadways (FGG171/3) which were their first production bodies, and one for an operator in Birmingham. The fourth was DAG607, new to Hill and Paterson of A1 Service, Ardrossan in February 1950 as a 35 seat coach with fleet number 29A, and was the last new half-cab single decker supplied to an A1 member. In 1960 it was sold to Gordon Brothers of Lamlash, and passed with the business to AC Lennox in February 1961, Lennox Transport in 1964 and The Arran Transport and Trading Company formed in January 1967 with new directors, but with Jack Lennox as omnibus operations manager. Sold to the dealer Irvine (Tiger Coaches) of Salsburgh in 1969, it then became a contractor's bus. It was photographed leaving Brodick on the 9.20 pm service to Whiting Bay on 26th July 1965, and still retains a radiator with the stripes which were the hallmark of vehicles in the fleet of its original owner.

Another rare chassis to receive a Scottish Aviation body was the Foden PVSC, introduced in 1945 with the Gardner engine as standard. Three of these emerged from the factory in 1948, although the company claimed that 44 were on order and the reduction was due to Government restrictions being made at the time. The first (SB7369) was in May for Dunoon Motor Services, the next with a five cylinder engine the following month for Tennant of Forth, and in August CCS61 which was a demonstrator. This was followed in December by CSD96 a Foden double decker demonstrator featured on page 28. With 32 coach seats, it joined the fleet of Thomas Hunter of Springside, also a member of A1 Service, in December 1948, who owned it for sixteen years, although it was actually stored for the last two. Just acquired and repainted into the striking livery of DE and DS Bannatyne of Blackwaterfoot, it was photographed at Brodick Pier on 27th July 1965, waiting for its departure at 11.05 am to Blackwaterfoot via the String Road, a service Bannatyne Motors had operated from its formation in April 1952 when it took over the route from Ribbeck's Motors of Brodick. With a six cylinder engine and re-seated with 35 service bus seats, it gave good service to the company, being finally withdrawn at the end of September 1971, at which time two of the three Scottish Aviation bodied Albion Victors in the fleet were still on the road.

Bannatyne Motors had another uncommon vehicle at that time, also with a body built by a Scottish company with a short production span, in this case from 1947-1951. Brockhouse of Clydebank constructed bodies on fourteen Maudslay Marathon 111s in 1949. Two were for McAteer of Dumbarton, and the remainder with full fronted bodies for Young's Bus Service of Paisley (XS6658-63/705-8) and two for AA Motor Services member JB Young of Ayr, one of which (CSD276) was bought by Young's of Paisley after only a month. These eleven coaches then passed to Western SMT in January 1951 and were given fleet numbers 2189-99. Coincidentally, two further Maudslays XS6983-4 with Scottish Aviation bodies were also taken over as 2200-1 and also ended up on Bute. After initial allocation to Kilmarnock and Johnstone Depots for use on the Glasgow to London service, they were all transferred to Rothesay in 1958 with the exception of 2192 which was scrapped after an accident. They ran there for a further two years, and apart from XS6706, were then sold to the dealer Millburn Motors in Glasgow. XS6706 was delicensed in April 1960, and unusually sold directly to Bannatyne Motors in October, and was withdrawn at the end of 1964. The Bannatyne fleet always showed great variety, the majority of vehicles being elderly second hand coaches, and XS6706 was unusual in having a 7.7 litre AEC engine, a quieter alternative to the Gardner. It was photographed in its final role as a shed at Shiskine Post Office, and features the "Bannatyne thistle" an emblem derived from a toffee manufacturer's wrapper.

Another Brockhouse bodied vehicle on Arran at that time was CSD711, Foden PVSC 6 with a 6 cylinder Gardner engine. One of only three Fodens to receive Brockhouse bodies, the first two in 1948 (SB7303-4) were delivered to Dunoon Motor Services, and CSD711 in August 1949 to Andrew Hunter of Springside, a member of A1 Service, Ardrossan. The body style was based on the design used by Alexander for its fleet of Leyland Cheetah chassis which entered service during 1938-39 and was developed to supply bodies for the parent company after the war when there was an oversupply of new chassis with a delay in obtaining bodies. CSD711 was sold to the newly-formed Lennox Transport in July 1964 joining Brockhouse bodied Leyland Comet DAG64, and passed to the Arran Trading and Transport Company (Arran Coaches) based at Whiting Bay in January 1967. It was withdrawn in March 1969 and replaced by GJS888, a Duple Midland bodied Bedford SB1 new to Mitchell of Stornoway, and sold to the dealer Irvine of Salsburgh. It was photographed at Lamlash garage on 27th July 1965, with "Lennox" in the destination box replacing that of A. Hunter the original owner with which it entered service, and still retained its original destination screen on the nearside. Arran Coaches incorporated both Lennox Transport of Whiting Bay with nine vehicles and Lennox Motors of Brodick with two coaches, and in August 1969 having sold the Lamlash garage, moved their office to the Pier at Brodick and relegated the ex-Lennox depot at Whiting Bay to the status of a store.

In addition to its Scottish Aviation bodied Foden, Bannatyne Motors ended up with three of the 23 Albion Victors model FT39N with bodies from the same company, all first licensed within a month of each other, and obtained from different operators late in their lives. The first to arrive was GVA635, photographed on Brodick Pier beside OUP934, one of Lennox Transport's three Duple bodied models. New to Duncan of Law in September 1951, GVA635 was sold to Hutchison of Overtown in 1954, passing to Garnock Valley Motors of Kilbirnie in 1958, and on to Bannatyne Motors the following year. Taken out of service in 1970, it later passed to McPherson of Donisthorpe for preservation. NWE663, new to Talbot Transport of Sheffield, joined the Bannatyne fleet in 1963, and LAO160, new to Young of Aspatria, arrived via Turnbull (Blue Band) of Lockerbie in 1966, both being withdrawn by 1972. OUP934 also reached Arran by a circuitous route, being new to Gardiner Brothers of Spennymoor in December 1953, via Rae of Borland and Pentland of Loanhead, passing to Lennox Transport in 1963 who operated it for four years. The other Duple bodied Albions (JVA890-1) in the Lennox fleet both came from Hutchison of Overtoun: 890 via King of Kirkcowan which was scrapped in 1966 and 891 which came directly and was dismantled for spares in 1963.

In addition to two Albions, one Foden and an 11 seater Austin J2BA OCS362, Bannatyne Motors in 1965 had a Leyland Comet KOF29, which like Lennox Transport's DAG64 also had an unusual body, this time constructed by Burlingham. As with Bannatyne's other acquisitions, KOF29 had previous owners, being new to Eatonways of Birmingham in March 1950, via Hynds of Paisley, finally arriving on Arran in 1961 from Wilson of Helensburgh. Photographed arriving at Brodick from Kildonan on 26th July 1965, it was withdrawn six months later, and sold to a dealer in Carmyle for scrap. Bannatyne's network had developed from its initial service from Brodick to Blackwaterfoot via the String Road to a south island circular service when it acquired the business of Donald Stewart of Corriecravie on 27th March 1960. He had garages at Whiting Bay and Corriecravie which were disposed of, and services from Low Kildonan to Whiting Bay and Brodick to Corriecravie, extended to Blackwaterfoot in July and August. The service network was further enhanced with the purchase of Weir's business in 1966 which resulted in a south island run from Brodick to Blackwaterfoot via Low Kildonan and Lagg, and a service to Lochranza via the String Road, Shiskine, Blackwaterfoot and Machrie. There was also an extensive tours program, but bus usage continued to fall during the late sixties, and with the end of visits to Lochranza from the *Duchess of Hamilton* in 1971, the subsequent car ferry service from Claonaig yielded little passenger transport. Accordingly, the business was finally sold to the Arran Trading and Transport Company on 30th September 1973 with a couple of Harrington bodied AEC Reliances EHD968/71 and a Ford Transit CSJ438L.

Historically, services round the north end of the island had been operated by the buses of EK Ribbeck & Sons based at Invercloy Garage, Brodick, the oldest surviving transport concern on the island. It started in 1879 with a mail car from Brodick to Corrie which was replaced with a motor bus in 1919 extending the service to Sannox. This was further extended to Lochranza in 1926 and to Catacol in 1930. The last year of operation was 1966, as the business was sold to Lennox Transport of Whiting Bay on 30th May. On paper, the fleet at that time consisted of five vehicles which were "runners" and two which were out of use. The operational fleet consisted of Plaxton bodied Commer Avenger SJ1298, photographed between Machrie and Blackwaterfoot on a round island tour. These always went anti-clockwise to aid traffic management. It was new to the company in April 1950 and passed to Lennox Transport, but was never repainted, delicensed in July 1966, and sold to the dealer Irvine of Salsburgh in November. Also transferred was Albion CHH740 illustrated on the front inside page, Commer SJ1325 featured on the front cover which was on semi-permanent hire, but in fact still licensed to McMillan of Pirnmill, Duple bodied Bedford SB SW8437 which was repainted and survived until May 1968, and 61DUP a 11 seat Morris J2BM which was used for a month before being converted for non-PSV use.

The two vehicles in the Ribbeck fleet which passed to Lennox Transport in May 1966 which were not operated were JAO748, a Scottish Aviation bodied Commer Q4 obtained from Weir of Machrie in 1961, identical to their CSD178 and GUS129, and Plaxton bodied Commer Commando SJ1189, parked at Brodick after a private hire. Coincidentally, a Harrington bodied Commer Commando SJ1190 new to Robertson of Blackwaterfoot which passed to McMillan of Pirnmill had also been operated by Ribbeck between 1961 and 1964. JAO748 was delicensed by the date of the sale and remained at Ribbeck's garage. SJ1189 ironically failed in service five days before the takeover and was subsequently scrapped. With the departure of Ribbeck's fleet from the roads of Arran, an iconic livery was no more, and the swallow motif which appeared on the sides of their coaches, and on the drivers' blazers, disappeared forever. Five of the island operators had already disappeared since 1959 when McMillan ceased, followed by Stewart in 1960, Gordon in 1961 and both AC Lennox of Whiting Bay and Lennox Motors of Brodick in 1964. Weir was to follow in June, Lennox Transport in 1967, and finally Bannatyne Motors in 1973, leaving Arran Transport and Trading Company as the sole bus operator on the island. With the lifting of the ban on vehicles wider than 7'6" the first underfloor engined bus arrived on Arran in 1968, SHO801 a Duple Midland bodied AEC Reliance with semi-automatic transmission, and a new era in transport on the island had arrived.

The trains from Glasgow Central Station were linked to the workings of the ferry from Ardrossan to Brodick, and the town of Ardrossan was supplied by the buses of Western SMT and the three Ayrshire independent companies, A1 Service of Ardrossan, AA Motor Services of Ayr and Clyde Coast Services. This photograph, taken at the junction of Princes Street and Glasgow Street on 24th May 1964, shows representatives of all three companies. Clyde Coast Crossley EO8789, owned by member George McGregor of Saltcoats, is leading the way. One of five new to Barrow Corporation in 1948 with "Mancunian" style Crossley bodies to operate for Clyde Coast, it arrived in September 1958. Dodds of Troon fitted it with a reconditioned Gardner 6LW engine in 1959, and it was the last to be withdrawn in July 1967 and sold for scrap. McGregor also bought EO8795 which was re-engined, and 8792 which passed to fellow member Shields three years later. Behind is AA member Dodds of Troon Guy Arab 11 OSD178, which started life in 1944 as Plymouth Corporation CDR757 with a utility Roe lowbridge body, arriving in Troon in December 1954. It eventually entered service in June 1960 re-registered, with a Northern Counties 64 seat body. With an 8 feet wide body on a 7'6" wide chassis the combination proved to be unstable, and it required to have three of the 37 seats on the top deck removed. It was eventually sold to Millburn Motors in February 1973. At the rear is A1 member Thomas Hunter of Springside Daimler CVG6LX RAG578 (fleet number 19) new in December 1960 with a Northern Counties 73 seat body to a similar "Southdown" design, and the first 30 feet long bus in the company. It was delicensed in January 1973, but still survives today in preservation

Left: Of the four members of Clyde Coast Services which survived until the 1960s, Hogarth of Ardrossan ceased operating on 30th April 1966, and Shields of Saltcoats in June 1971. On 1st April 1988 the two remaining companies, Frazer of Fairlie and McGregor of Saltcoats, merged with vehicles now licensed to Clyde Coast Services operating out of McGregor's depot at Ardrossan. Their service from Saltcoats to Largs via West Kilbride passed through Ardrossan and Fairlie, terminating at Barr Crescent at the north end of Largs. The individual fleets had always shown much variety, and the first new vehicle for the group to be purchased after the war was a highbridge all Leyland PD1 BAG43 licensed to Frazer in April 1946. Reliable, although underpowered, it ran for 20 years, and was photographed beside the garage at Fairlie on 25th July 1965. By then looking less than immaculate, it was sold the following year to Codona, a dealer in Carmyle and scrapped. In January 1948 it was joined by a further identical vehicle BSD598, although the body on this Leyland was constructed by Samlesbury Engineering in Lancashire under sub contract, due to the high demand for Leyland products at that time. It had a shorter life as it was withdrawn after an accident in May 1963, and dismantled for spares. It was replaced by CCK621, an all Leyland PD2 which had the more powerful 9.8 litre engine, and was new to Ribble Motor Services in 1948. It was withdrawn in December 1966.

Right: When London Transport started to withdraw their post-war double deckers, they were eagerly snapped up by operators big and small, and the Ayrshire independents were no exception. Clyde Coast ended up with 3 RTs, 5 RTLs and 1 RTW, although because of transfers between individual members and acquisitions from A1 Services which provided five, only three came direct from London Transport. One RTL had been previously operated by Samuel Ledgard of Leeds, and the RTLs were operated by only one member of Clyde Coast. The first RTL to appear with Clyde Coast was JXC20 which was photographed at Saltcoats, waiting to depart for Largs. It had entered service in Scotland with A1 member James Reid of Saltcoats in March 1959, passing to Shields of Saltcoats in September 1963. It was finally sold for scrap in 1969. As the prototype RTL, it was new to London Transport in June 1948, entering service as RTL501 because numbers 1-500 were originally kept for the 8 feet wide Leylands which entered service as RTW1-500. Supposed to have a Metro-Cammell body, it appeared with a Park Royal one which was intended for RT657, as was the registration number JXC20. It was the only RTL to enter service with a roof box, and unusually retained the same body at overhauls in 1952 and 1955, only finally losing its roof box when it arrived in Scotland.

Western SMT competed with Clyde Coast with their through service from Kilmarnock to Largs which was extended to Greenock in June 1956, but it was the sole operator into Largs from the east with the former Youngs of Paisley service from Glasgow via Kilbirnie. This started in the late 1920s and passed to Western SMT on takeover in 1951. At that time there were two depots in Largs, one at Allanpark with origins in the Western SMT service from Glasgow to Largs via Renfrew. The other was the ex Youngs garage on Main Street, which could only accommodate six buses. Accordingly, a new depot was constructed adjacent to this in 1953 which was rebuilt in 1979 and survived until 1995. At different times, it was a subdepot of Johnstone or Greenock, and in the sixties both. Later under Clydeside ownership it had its own paper allocation. In the seventies Johnstone provided nine specified buses when this photograph of JB2421 (MAH500E) was taken, crawling up the notorious Haylie Brae on the 4.23 17 service to Glasgow on 17th March 1975. One of the 36 Bristol FLFs obtained in the NBC "swap" with the unloved SBG Bristol VRTs, in this case KB2242 (NCS435G) which in fact went in error to Lincolnshire RCC. MAH500E had arrived from Eastern Counties OC and entered service at Johnstone Depot in Tilling Red colours in August 1973. Repainted at Kilmarnock in April 1974, it retained its original destination display so that a standard Western blind had to be trimmed to fit the available width leading to the restricted destination detail seen in this picture. Unsuitable for OMO operation, it was prematurely delicensed in August 1979 and sold for scrap in March 1981. The other vehicles allocated to Largs at that time were similar JB2416/20, Alexander bodied Daimler Fleetlines JR2144-9 (JAG497-502F) converted for OMO operation, and a spare Leyland Leopard.

In 1965 Clyde Hover Ferries introduced the world's first all year round Hovercraft service from the beach at the north end of Largs to Millport. With a journey time of only eleven minutes it could carry 38 passengers, but after considerable financial losses, it ceased operation after only a year. It was photographed arriving at Millport on 28th July 1965, where the local bus services on Cumbrae which were operated by Millport Motors terminated at the pier. The first service on the island running to Keppel Pier on the west side of the island had been started in 1933 by John Morrison, with the business trading as Morrison Brothers the following year This became Millport Motors Ltd in 1951, a company which survives to this day. In 1972 a car ferry service commenced from Largs to a new slipway at the north end of the island at the site of the old "Tattie Pier" termed the "Cumbrae Slip" and a bus service transported passengers the three miles to Millport Pier. Prior to that, services were confined to the south end of the island, linking the golf course and caravan site with the Old Pier and Keppel Pier. The former was first opened in 1833, rebuilt in 1991 and is still in use today. Keppel Pier was built in 1888 as a secondary pier to take pressure off the Old Pier, and was used for longer distance excursions, but finally closed in 1971. Photographed there in 1965 are Albion DAG983 and Commer SJ1315. The senior secondary school for Cumbrae after the war was still Rothesay Academy, and scholars were ferried from Keppel Pier and the Old Pier over to Fairlie Pier on the mainland and then on to Bute by bus and ferry from Wemyss Bay.

There were only two full size buses on Cumbrae by 1965, and two eleven seater Fords which ran between the golf course and the caravan site via the Old Pier. Both microbuses were purchased new, CVS599 in 1963 and EVS872B in 1964, but both had left the island by 1972. Two second hand Bedford OBs had operated between 1954 and 1963 and a Scottish Aviation bodied Commer Q4 between 1960 and 1963, but the only new bus purchased until 1972 was SJ1315, a similar Commer Q4 in 1950. An unusual purchase in 1964 was DAG983, an Albion Victor model FT39N with a Scottish Aviation body, similar to the three which ran for Bannatyne Motors on Arran, but without the full front. It was new to Paterson of Dalry in May 1950 and was the third example of this model of Albion out of a total of 23 to receive this body. They were all built during 1950 and 1951, but it was one of only five to be sold to Scottish operators. All were fitted with 31 coach seats apart from an export version with dual doors. It arrived on Cumbrae in 1964, and was used for tours and ferry connections until sold in 1967 to a contractor in Peterhead. It was photographed arriving back at the Old Pier on the connecting service from Keppel Pier via the housing scheme.

Scottish Aviation bodied Commer Q4 SJ1315 operated on Cumbrae for sixteen years, longer than any other bus had on the island. It was also photographed on a typically wet day at the Old Pier in July 1965. New in June 1950, it was one of 33 Commers of this model which received Scottish Aviation bodies between 1948 and 1950. The chassis were new as wartime goods vehicles which were rebuilt and re-bodied as coaches, and were sold to operators all over Scotland, with only one going south of the border to Hartness of Penrith (JAO748.) It later ended up on Arran with Weir of Machrie. In addition to SJ1315, two other coaches were sold to island operators, SJ1261 to Newton of Brodick and SJ1325 to Robertson of Blackwaterfoot. The other Commer Q4 which ran on Cumbrae was CCS926, also new to Paterson of Dalry, and delivered in March 1949. It was sold to AC Lennox of Whiting Bay in 1955, passing to Millport Motors in 1960, but only ran for a further three years. SJ1315 was not withdrawn until 1966 when it was sold to a dealer in Carmyle. Scottish Aviation also produced bodies for the popular Commer Commando chassis, and 32 entered service in 1949, of which 28 were for Alexander of Falkirk and Lawson of Kirkintilloch. With light alloy bodies using materials derived from those used in aircraft construction, they resulted in sturdy and economical coaches, ideal for the poorly finished roads in many parts of Scotland at that time.

On the adjacent island of Bute, Western SMT had a policy of only operating full size vehicles since taking over the services of the Rothesay Tramways Company in November 1949 with its fleet of 25 elderly vehicles. An Albion Victor and a Bedford WLB were immediately disposed of, and a Bedford WTB in 1954, all having only 20 seats. Thereafter the allocation varied, with an influx of elderly double deckers to cover the busy summer season, but the usual allocation was around a dozen double deckers plus fifteen single deckers. It came as a surprise therefore when 28 seat Bedford VAS AYS736B arrived on the island in March 1971, remaining for seven years. No other small bus was to be allocated under Western ownership. One of four former MacBrayne's vehicles to enter the Western fleet in October 1970 when its Ardrishaig-based operation passed to the control of Thornliebank Depot, it alone was immediately transferred away to Dumfries Depot after being painted into Western's dual purpose cream and red livery, and given fleet number E4. On hearing of its arrival on Bute, we arranged to take our three month old daughter over for the day, and ended up having to drive straight on to the ferry as she was having a feed at the time, but were met by the sight of AYS736B parked on Rothesay Pier. Later transferred to Cumnock Depot to operate the experimental "ruralink" service from Dalmellington to Ballochmyle Hospital, it was sold in October 1979 to the Second Cumnock Boys Brigade and ended up still being garaged in Western's Cumnock Depot.

A motley collection of elderly re-bodied Leylands were cascaded down to Western's Bute operation during the fifties until the single decker fleet was largely replaced by twelve Maudslays in 1958. For the 1960 summer season, a management decision was made to replace the entire Rothesay allocation with a standardised modern fleet, and fifteen three year old Bristol LSG6s, T1269-83 (JSD905-19) uniquely fitted with Alexander dual purpose bodies arrived. They were fitted with 41 fixed leather coach type seats, and most remained until withdrawn in autumn 1970. They were delivered new to Inchinnan (1269-73) and Greenock (1274-83) depots for the Largs via Renfrew service which required single deckers because of a low bridge at Langbank. 1277-83 however had mysteriously arrived in service bus livery. The Greenock vehicles had subsequently spent a year in Dumfries and Galloway on long distance work, but all now settled down to a different life on island tours and services such as the steep climb to Canada Hill. All were eventually converted for OMO operation from 1967 onwards by the primitive method of fitting a manual door control linkage to the one-piece door with a large handle. Their replacements were from a batch of Bristol MW6Gs, T1387-1406 (LCS197-216) new in 1958 with identical bodies but with two piece folding doors and a revised frontal design incorporating a grille to aid air flow to the engine. LCS209 came from Johnstone Depot in November 1970, and was photographed at Rhubodach in September 1971, awaiting passengers off the ferry from Colintraive. It was withdrawn in February 1975, later operating for Bebb of Llantwit.

The replacement double decker fleet which came in 1960 turned out to be D340-51 (BCS301-312) thirteen year old all Leyland PD1s which had previously operated on the high intensity routes out of Thornliebank Depot. BCS302 was photographed in September 1965 at Pointhouse Garage in Ardbeg, the former Rothesay Tramways depot which houses the West Coast Motors Bute allocation to this day. It had undergone a major body overhaul in April 1960, was delicensed on 30th September 1966 and sold to the dealer Millburn Motors and scrapped. The entire batch (BCS301-325) was allocated to Thornliebank from new, and BCS313-325 remained until withdrawn in 1964-65. The Rothesay vehicles, operating a lower mileage on flat roads, survived longer, and BCS306-9 continued in service until 20 years old, being withdrawn on 31st March 1967. They outlived every double decker of every make which entered service with Western after the war until 1953, except for yet another motley collection which replaced them on Bute. These were four Leyland PD1s from 1949 re-bodied in 1952, four all Leyland highbridge PD2s new to Youngs of Paisley in 1950, and four ex London wartime Guy Arabs re-bodied in 1954. All had also been withdrawn by the end of that year. The final group of double deckers to arrive were twelve assorted Leyland PD2/20s with Northern Counties bodies new in 1955-7, of which seven surprisingly had platform doors. The last double decker to leave the island was D1187 (HCS966) on 30th September 1971 which was the first bus delivered new to Western with doors. The replacements for the next decade were 49 seat Leyland Leopards. These included the first vehicles to arrive in black and white coach colours since the fifties, L2224/31 (OAG528/35H) in June 1972, and the first new buses on Bute since AEC Regals SJ1048-50 were delivered in 1946, L2491-2 (SCS360-1M) in 1974.

Further north, Loch Lomond was another popular destination for day trips from Glasgow and the surrounding conurbations, and the "Luss bus" taking passengers from Balloch to the scenic village on the west shore of Loch Lomond was busy, particularly at the weekends. Accordingly, a double decker was rostered for the service which ran eight times a day on weekdays, but thirteen on a Saturday when the last bus to leave Balloch was at 10.30 pm. Central SMT operated it from their Dunbartonshire depot at Old Kilpatrick, and in 1965 had allocated an "odd" bus, FVA546 (L442) which was photographed at Balloch Bus Station on 23rd July 1965. On paper this was a standard Northern Counties bodied Leyland PD2 new in 1951, but it arrived out of sequence and was given an isolated registration number and fleet number out of numerical context. Delivered new to Wishaw Depot, it moved to Gavinburn Depot at Old Kirkpatrick in 1959 where it remained for nine years after which it was sold to the dealer Irvine of Salsburgh. It then passed on to Northern Roadways who repainted it into their green colours, and ran it for a further year. The full batch of Northern Counties bodied Leylands consisted of CVD302-341, FVA546 with fleet numbers L302-341,442 with the first 31 being PD1s and the remainder PD2s. However, the body style differed according to the date of construction, and the final arrivals L323-332 had the more modern 4 bay design with "standee" windows. L322/33-40 and 442 also had the extra windows as seen in this photograph, where L442 is in the later style of livery with a single cream band.

The other popular destination for those arriving at Balloch was the scenic village of Balmaha on the eastern shore of Loch Lomond. This could be reached by a boat trip from Balloch, or on the buses of AC Barrie, who was the proprietor of "Loch Lomond Coaches" based in the nearby village of Ballagan. The service has survived in its basic form until today, albeit having been in the hands of many operators, latterly as a secured service, as with the route to Luss. Traditionally a vehicle from Barrie's coach fleet was allocated to the Balmaha service with an additional second hand bus acquired to provide help over the summer, which was sold on at the end of the season. In 1965, the unlikely vehicle was a Burlingham bodied AEC Regal GSF694 (B375) new to SMT in July 1949, which was photographed parked in the depot in July 1965. With a sliding door, and high backed coach seats, it was not the obvious choice for such a service, and had spent the last ten years of its life based at Galashiels Depot operating poorly patronised services in the Scottish Borders. It was withdrawn in October 1965 and sold to the dealer Locke in Edinburgh from whom Barrie had purchased it. It was then sold on in November to a contractor Baird in Port Glasgow, who used it on contract work in Girvan.

The regular vehicle allocated to Barrie's service from Balloch to Balmaha at the beginning of 1965 was ASN777B, a Ford Thames 30 with a 41 seat Duple Northern Firefly body. It was new in December 1964 and converted for OMO operation with a driver operated door. In March it was promoted to the role of a full coach, and replaced by a unique vehicle featured at the 1963 Scottish Motor Show. This was BWG650B, an Albion Viking demonstrator model VK41L with a Leyland 370 vertical front engine. All subsequent Albion Vikings were to have rear engines. It entered service with Alexander Midland at Perth Depot in August 1964 with fleet number MN16, but it did not find favour with the Scottish Bus Group and was returned to Albion Motors the following year. Converted for OMO operation, and with a luggage pen on the nearside behind the passenger door, it was ideal for the Balmaha service. It was replaced in December 1967 by JSN888F, a Ford R192 with a Willowbrook body and 45 dual purpose seats, which later operated in Shropshire with Valley Motors of Bishops Castle. BWG650B ended up on the Isle of Lewis with Lochs of Crossbost, operating the Stornoway to Ranish service for the next ten years.

The extra bus for the 1964 summer season had been HWS938 which arrived in May from the local dealer Millburn Motors of Glasgow. An AEC Regal IV, it was new to Western SMT in 1951 in a batch of "London Coaches" HWS927-940 (A920-933.) These were diverted from SMT to provide competition with Northern Roadways who had ordered a fleet of 20 coaches with Burlingham Seagull bodies for their express services. The Western vehicles had 30 seat Alexander bodies with reclining seats and toilets, and operated the London service until replaced by lightweight Guy Arab coaches in 1955. Their toilets were then removed and they were reseated, with 920-1/6-7/9-30 receiving 44 bus seats and the remainder 40 dual purpose seats. The six with bus seats plus 932 were then transferred to Cumnock Depot to operate the Glasgow to Dumfries service, and transferred to Highland Omnibuses in 1964 (as were GSF690/2/5-6 similar to 694 on page 22.) The remainder moved to Inchinnan Depot initially to operate Western's share of the Glasgow to Manchester service. All were then rebuilt to varying degrees, such that no two looked the same, the most radical revision work being on HWS938. First it had all its chrome trim and the front bumper bar removed in 1958 with the fitting of a rectangular panel, later replaced in March 1961 by a "Bristol MW" style grille. Little real use was found for them at Inchinnan Depot as time went by and HWS938 was stored from September 1962, delicensed in August 1963 and sold to Millburn Motors in February 1964. In September 1964 it returned to Millburn Motors and passed to Greyhound of Arbroath who promptly returned it. In June 1965, it was sold to Campion of Clonmel and after an accident ended up as a site hut for a contractor there.

Further north on the east bank of Loch Lomond, is the jetty at Inversnaid, with ferries plying across the loch to Tarbet and Inveruglas. Five miles east of Inversnaid is the hamlet of Stronachlachar, with its pier at the west end of Loch Katrine, and connecting them is the single track road road which runs alongside Loch Arklet. The steamship *Sir Walter Scott*, built by Denny Bros at Dumbarton in 1899, still undertakes cruises on Loch Katrine sailing from Trossachs Pier at the east end, and both it and a cruise ship also visit Stronachlachar. In 1965, Loch Lomond-Loch Katrine Services operated two full size buses and a minibus, and provided a connecting service which was an integral part of a circular tour from Glasgow. Photographed at Stronachlachar, collecting passengers from the cruise ship, is Leyland TS7 RN7765, new to Ribble Motor Services in 1936, and re-bodied with an 8 feet wide Duple body in 1950 and re-engined. Sold to the Preston branch of Millburn Motors in 1961, it came north and operated this service until September 1966 when 30 years old. In the foreground of the picture is BRN859, a Leyland PS1 also new to Ribble, but one of the last batch (BRN857-863) of this model purchased by the company, as late as 1949, with 7' 6'' wide Burlingham bodies. It was sold to Milburn Motors in 1960 but did not enter service with its new operator until 1962. Withdrawn at the same time, it was sold to a dealer in Comrie for scrap. Although only having the less powerful 7.4 litre engines, they had 31 well spaced coach seats, and only crawled in convoy along the narrow road. It was surprising not to have both vehicles of narrow width.

At Tarbet, MacTavish of Arrochar provided a connection for passengers wishing to travel to the pier at Arrochar and join the cruise vessel on Loch Long. Awaiting the arrival of the paddle steamer *Maid of the Loch* is ex-MacBrayne's Maudslay GUS408 parked beside it is Plaxton bodied Bedford SB FBA926 new to Fieldsend of Salford in 1952. The other vehicles in the fleet were two 13 seat Trojans and a 19 seat Duple Midland bodied Bedford, J2SZ2. GUS408 was one of 16 Maudslay Marathons new in 1949 with 35 seat Park Royal coach bodies, almost identical in design to the three AEC Regals delivered to MacBrayne's in 1937 which were seized by the War Department three years later. The first six (GUS407-412) had fleet numbers 19/21/31-2/4/49 which took up vacant spaces, while the remainder (GUS924-933) became 134-143. GUS930-933 unusually had large mail compartments seating only 27 passengers and GUS930 and 933 were re-bodied by Duple in 1959, with GUS 933 joining the MacTavish fleet in 1968. With the exception of GUS931 and 932 all of the remainder of these sister Maudslays were rebuilt between 1958 and 1960. The work, which involved replacing the side windows with rubber mountings, was carried out on GUS408 by Bennett of Glasgow. Thereafter it continued to run out of the Glasgow Depot in Lancefield Street on duplicate journeys to and from Ardrishaig until withdrawn in November 1963. Macintosh licensed it in June 1964 and it ran for a further seven years, later joined by another two MacBrayne's vehicles which had been re-bodied by Duple. These were Maudslay FGA159 (15) paired with FGB418 (35), in 1968 and AEC Royal KGG708 (12) paired with KGG709 (27) which was acquired in 1970.

Further west with spectacular views over the Kyles of Bute are the scenic villages of Kames and Tighnabruaich, popular as a location for holiday homes and a weekend cruising destination. The Kyles of Bute Bus Company operated services between these villages connecting with the steamers, and also from Kames to Millhouse, Otter Ferry and Ardlamont. There was also a shoppers service to Glasgow on the first Wednesday of each month, and to Dunoon on Fridays and Saturdays. George Chisholm of Bearsden had acquired the licences of the company with its five buses on 1st April 1965, the legal address being "Auchenlochan Pier, Kames." Between January 1967 and 1968, Colin McColl & Sons of Tighnabruaich took over the services using three Chisholm coaches, having applied to acquire the licences, but they were never transferred. The three vehicles were 41 seat Ford Trooper BSN305C, 29 seat Duple coach bodied Bedford VAS BSN520C and Burlingham bodied Bedford SB8 JVD770. Duple bodied Bedford SB5 BSN281C which Chisholm kept at Bearsden had passed to Whitelaw of Bearsden in May 1966. Finally in May 1970, Gorman of Dunoon acquired the services and vehicles. The regular vehicle on the local service in 1965 was AEC Regal JXK140, new (with JXK141) in June 1947 to Glenton Coaches with a rare 26 seat Vincent coach body. This was replaced in 1956 with a Plaxton 30 seat body and the vehicle later sold locally to Taylor of Meppershall, from whom it was acquired in October 1963. Withdrawn in August 1966, it was sold to the contractor Baird of Port Glasgow who used it for staff transport.

Back on the Firth of Clyde, serving the sailing communities of Helensburgh and Rhu, was Garelochead Coaches based at Bromley Garage in Helensburgh with its principal service from Helensburgh to Garelochead via Rhu and Shandon. This service was started in 1919 by Henry Brown, trading as Brown's Motor Service of Helensburgh, and the company built up over the years by the Brown family. On 2nd June 1951 it was sold with a collection of fourteen elderly buses to the Foy family who operated coaches in Glasgow and set about updating the fleet. John Foy had just acquired what became a unique vehicle, a demonstrator for Scottish Aviation which had emerged from the factory at Prestwick in December 1948 registered CSD96, and with the first double deck body constructed by the company. A Foden PVD6 with platform doors, it was exhibited at The Scottish Motor Show in 1949, but first registered in May 1951 as JGD675. Photographed at Garelochead in July 1965 correctly numbered 13, it was withdrawn in June 1968 and is now preserved by The East Midland Transport Society. Scottish Aviation only built another 20 double deck bodies, all for Glasgow Corporation, five on Albion CX37S chassis, five on Daimler CVD6 chassis, and ten on pre-war AEC Regents, all during 1950. Mysteriously, a Leyland TD3 WJ9091 (R322) acquired by Alexander with a damaged body from Sheffield Corporation in 1941 but never operated, was sent to Metal Sections in Birmingham for a new body frame. It then appeared at Prestwick in November 1947, possibly as a template for a new double deck body, but returned unused to Larbert and was scrapped.

A number of local services were also operated by the company including Helensburgh to Luss, Garelochead to Whistlefield and the Helensburgh town services, in addition to school contracts and contract services for the Faslane and Coulport Naval establishments. There was also a service to Coulport via Clynder taken over from Irvine of Kilcreggan. In 1952 an application was made to run this service through to Glasgow as a replacement for Clyde steamer services which were beginning to be withdrawn, but Central SMT and British Railways objected. At the end of 1963, three AEC Mark IV Regals were obtained from London Transport for this service. Ideally suited to the narrow roads, they were from the first batch of RFs only 27'6" long and 7'6" wide with Metro Cammell 35 seat bodies, and were already converted for OMO operation. All subsequent members of the RF class were built to the newly announced 30 feet length, and RF1-25 remained unique. With glazed roof panels, they were primarily used on tour work, being first licensed for the Festival of Britain in 1951, but all withdrawn in 1963 when a shortage of drivers led to the end of this work. LUC 214-5/24, formerly RF14-5/24 with Garelochead fleet numbers 39-41 operated the Coulport service for four years. LUC215 photographed near Clynder in July 1965 had entered service in January 1964 and was withdrawn in March 1968 and scrapped. LUC 214 only survived until 1966, but LUC224 continued until October 1968. It was withdrawn for spares in June 1966, but recertified and appeared with 41 service bus seats in March 1968. These fine vehicles may have had short lives both in London and in Scotland, but proved very useful in their role on the roads of the Rosneath Peninsula between Gareloch and Loch Long.

Above Loch Long is Loch Goil and the remote picturesque village of Lochgoilhead where MacBrayne's garaged two small buses overnight. Historically it and nearby Carrick Castle could only be accessed by the daily steamer service from Gourock to Lochgoilhead via Carrick Castle. In October 1946 this was replaced by a bus service from Carrick Castle via Lochgoilhead, the B828 and Glen Mhor, the Rest and Be Thankful and Glen Croe to Arrochar Station, where it connected with trains to and from Glasgow and Fort William. MacBrayne's were granted a licence to operate a 14 seat vehicle although some of the roads were unsuited to the Bedfords allocated (1939 Bedford WLGs CGE200-2) and initially there were many problems. The steamer service was reinstated from June to September 1947, an ex-military Humber Snipe was re-bodied as a shooting brake to act as a shuttle, and it was only when road reconstruction was completed in 1948 that a reliable all year round service was established. Initially 14 seat Harkness bodied Thornycroft Nippies delivered new in 1948 with mail compartments were allocated and FGD4 (76) became the regular bus. From March 1957, 20 seaters were allowed and by 1962 the two regular buses on the service run were KGD905-6 (164-5.) New in 1952 with a lorry-based Bedford chassis the OLAZ, they had 20 seat Duple bodies with mail compartments, and were withdrawn in early 1966. The spare bus which was used on tours and provided duplicates on Fridays, had been HGG359 (149) a 20 seat Croft bodied Thornycroft Nippy sold to McLachlan of Tayvallich in June 1962. Photographed outside the depot in September 1965 are KGD905 off the service run and UGA616 (177.)

Ascending from the layby at the top of the "Rest and be Thankful" where it had collected passengers off the 7.00 am service from Campbeltown to Glasgow and the 9.00 service from Glasgow to Tarbert, is KGD905. Arriving at Lochgoilhead (Road End) the timetable terminus at the intersection of the single track road from Carrick Castle with the main A83 to Kintyre, it was photographed in May 1965 returning on the 10.55 service to Carrick Castle. The section between there and Arrochar Station had been discontinued. From August 1964, the second bus at Lochgoilhead was employed on a school contract to Inveraray via Hell's Glen, and newly-arrived Bedford VAS AYS736B (73) was surprisingly rostered. Seen on page 18 in Western ownership, it had a Willowbrook body with service bus seats, and remained in MacBrayne's Ardrishaig allocation until Western SMT took over. Sometimes there was also a third bus kept at Lochgoilhead, usually UGA616 seen on the previous page, although on that occasion it was deputising for AYS736B. UGA616 was MacBrayne's first C class Bedford with a forward-control truck chassis modified for PSV use, and classified as C4Z, it was the only 4 ton model to enter the fleet, and was the last with a petrol engine. With a 29 seat Duple body, it entered service in May 1958 and left North Uist for Mull in 1964 when MacBrayne's took over Cowe of Tobermory. It moved to Ardrishaig the following year as a spare bus and in the summer was used on tours from Ardrishaig to Rothesay. Delicensed in late 1969, it was sold to the contractor Laidlaw of Rutherglen.

Western SMT took over responsibility for the southern area services of MacBrayne's on 3rd October 1970, operating their Ardrishaig Depot as a sub-depot of Thornliebank, with the garage at Lochgoilhead, and a one bus shed at Inveraray. The Bedfords YYS174 (54) HGA985D (212) EGA834C (146) and AYS736B (73) were given fleet numbers E1-4. The first three were painted into Western's black and white coach colours with the "Royal Route" crest beside the door and "Royal Mail Services" in red lettering on the rear, E4 appeared in red and cream dual purpose livery. Five of the newest Leyland Leopards at Thornliebank Depot (KCS151-6F, ML2180-3/5-6) in black and white colours were kept overnight at Ardrishaig Depot, and OAG526-7H, ML2222-3) were also used when they arrived new. For the first week, Western continued to keep a Leopard where MacBrayne's had kept their "sleeper" at the BRS depot at Kinloch Road in Campbeltown to operate the 7.00 am service to Glasgow, but thereafter operated only to Tarbert with a connecting West Coast Motors coach to Campbeltown. The Glasgow departures continued from the MacBrayne's Bus Station in Parliamentary Road until 7th February 1971 when they moved down to Anderston Cross Bus Station. While E4 left Ardrishaig immediately, the other three Bedfords returned in Western colours, two for Lochgoilhead and the third (E2 or 3) operated the service from Ardrishaig to Oban. A Leopard, or Bedford in the school holidays, was parked at Inveraray overnight for the 7.40 service to Ardrishaig. However, the MacBrayne's garage on Barn Brae could not accommodate a full size bus, which was parked near the driver's home, and the garage was sold to a local garage company in 1976. Photographed on Saturday 6th March 1971 was E3 at the top of the "Rest and be Thankful" waiting to return to Carrick Castle after exchanging mail with ML2222 on the 8.20 service from Tarbert to Glasgow. Like the Western SMT coaches seen on page 35 and 52, it too had a serious accident, but unlike them, its original body was rebuilt, but fitted with 53 service bus seats from a withdrawn vehicle.

Western SMT, and Highland Omnibuses who took over most of the MacBrayne's bus operation, were anxious to dispose of the more remote services, and in April 1973 the Carrick Castle service passed to local businessman Douglas Campbell of Lochgoilhead with YYS174. The Hell's Glen school service had ceased in June 1971. YYS174 was the first of seven Duple coach bodied Bedford C5Zs new in May 1960, but uniquely fitted with a mail compartment for work on Islay, meeting the ferry from West Loch Tarbert to Port Ellen and Port Askaig. Identical 610CYS (186) joined it the following year. In May 1966 YYS174 was replaced by a new bus seated VAS HGA983D (210) and transferred to Ardrishaig to replace the OLAZs on the Lochgoilhead service. Photographed in June 1973 at the "Top of the Rest," it went on to have an illustrious career as Maggie's bus in the soap *Take the High Road*, and still in Western colours turned up in Bearsden in May 1979 to take my children from their school to the swimming pool. Later repainted back into MacBrayne's livery, using my slides as a guide, it returned to Western who used it on the seasonal service to Brodick Castle on Arran, and is now in private preservation. E2 and E3 were converted for OMO operation in 1976 leaving Ardrishaig in February 1977 when they were delicensed and stored at Cumnock Depot, leaving just before E4 arrived there for the "ruralink" service. A new local service in Erskine required a small bus so this pair were also repainted into cream and red colours, and transferred to Inchinnan Depot in March 1978, being finally withdrawn in 1980.

Ten miles beyond the Lochgoilhead Road End is the former royal burgh of Inveraray, where the bus services from Glasgow to and from Kintyre have always made a refreshment stop, and it was common to see a line-up of MacBrayne's service buses and coaches parked beside the pier. On Saturday 1st May 1965 at 11.30 am these were the coaches on the 9.00 departure from Glasgow with the regular vehicle 294AGE (53) running through to Tarbert, where McConnachie provided a connection on to Campbeltown. The last departure from Glasgow at 3.15 pm however went straight through to Campbeltown, an arrangement which had been agreed in 1940 when the Clyde and Campbeltown Shipping Company withdrew its cargo and passenger service from Campbeltown and Carradale. In July and August, the 9 am service continued to West Loch Tarbert to provide a connection with the 1.05 pm steamer to Islay. Beside it is 391FGB (189) acting as a duplicate to Ardrishaig, an almost daily requirement, particularly throughout the summer. Both vehicles were AEC Reliances with Duple Midland bodies, and MacBrayne's bought nineteen between 1959 and 1962. Sixteen were fitted with 41 or 43 coach seats, and provided a degree of comfort and elegance which Western's dual purpose Leyland Leopards could not match. Surprisingly three were fitted with 44 bus seats, albeit externally identical apart from one lacking skylight windows at the front. Both passed to Highland Omnibuses with the rest of the MacBrayne's fleet apart from E1-4, four Bedford VAS sold to island operators, and eighteen coaches which went to Alexander Midland. As Highland B52 and 60, they joined a large fleet of AEC Reliances used indiscriminately on a wide range of duties, and were withdrawn in 1977, with 52 providing spares for Morar Motors and 60 being scrapped. Also parked is Duple bodied 606CYS (182) on tour.

Inveraray at 11.30 on Sunday 29th April 1973 was more tranquil as Western SMT Leyland Leopard RSD732J (ML2341) awaits to depart for Tarbert but now screened for Campbeltown to indicate that there was a through connection. From the latest batch of Leyland Leopards to be allocated to Thornliebank Depot, (RSD 729-32J, ML2338-41,) 49 seat RSD732J new in April 1971 was as customary delivered in black and white colours, but had just returned from a repaint when photographed. However, its body was burnt out in June 1974 and it reappeared a year later in the same livery, but with a multibay 53 seat body with bus seats, which was intended for the last of the current order for that year. As such it continued to operate down to Tarbert, but was withdrawn in December 1980. Scheduled to go to Bute for the summer season, it was transferred up to Highland Omnibuses in February as their L4. Continuing to lead a nomadic life, in April 1982 it went on loan to Alexander Fife for two months, returned to the pool at Inverness, was sent up to the outstation at Dunbeath for a school contract to Wick, was withdrawn in October 1983, and passed to Alexander Midland for spares in December. It then appeared with Meredith of Malpas in February 1984, was acquired by Shearings of Wigan as a Driver Trainer with fleet number 1 and re-registered SPR35. When they sold their bus operation to their management, it was then re-registered TNA161J and was used in service with Timeline still in Shearing colours. Now preserved, it is back in Western colours with its original registration.

Twenty five miles down the A83 is Lochgilphead, the administrative centre of Argyll and Bute, and two miles further on is Ardrishaig where MacBrayne's had a garage since 1912. This was replaced by a new depot in 1929, the basic structure of which survives to this day. Even in the 1960s there was a local service between the two communities, with ten journeys on a weekday, and on 16th November 1968, Duple bodied Bedford VAS HGA987D (214) one of three coaches new in July 1966 for extended tours, was photographed approaching Ardrishaig on the 2.00 service from Lochgilphead. It was transferred to Alexander Midland as MW298 at Stepps Depot when MacBrayne's ended their Kintyre operation in October 1970, but was sold on to SMT Sales and Service in November 1971. Of the 24 Bedford VAS with Duple Bella Vista bodies purchased by MacBrayne's between 1962 and 1969, eighteen passed to Midland, but four were never operated, and sadly little use was found for the others. The two at Milngavie Depot were even regularly used on my local service into Glasgow. HGA987D had not, as was customary, been delicensed at Glasgow during the winter of 1968, and remained at Ardrishaig for private hires. The remainder of the Ardrishaig area allocation that day consisted of YYS174, AYS736B and UGA616 at Lochgoilhead, another VAS 847HUS (94) at Inveraray (EGA834C had not yet been allocated,) HGA985D on the Ardrishaig to Oban service, and three AEC Reliance coaches on the Glasgow service, one based at Campbeltown, and two from Ardrishaig Depot.

MacBrayne's did not have a monopoly on rural bus services in the area and in 1965 three other companies operated services into Lochgilphead. These were Malcolm Maclachlan from Tayvallich, Stag Garage from Ford, and MacDonald and MacLellan from Ormsary. In addition to the through service from Glasgow, MacBrayne's also operated twice a day to Oban. On Saturday 17th July 1965 Maudslay Marathon GUS930 (140) re-bodied in 1959 with a Duple coach body awaits AEC Reliance 198CUS (63) which has just arrived as a duplicate on the 9.00 service from Glasgow. It will depart on the 1.15 service to Oban returning at 5.00 pm. The bus stance at Lochgilphead was the meeting point for the peripheral services, and MacLachlan's Morris Commercial SB7600 is waiting to return to Tayvallich. New to McLarty of Lochgilphead it had a rare 25 seat Willenhall body, and continued in service until December 1967. While it had a rare body, that on MacDonald and MacLellan's USP328 was unique. A Morris LD02M, it was fitted with a fourteen seat body by the bus operator McLennan of Spittalfield who only ever constructed fourteen bodies on new chassis, of which twelve were for its own fleet. It is believed to have been ordered by another operator, but came new to Ardrishaig in 1958, and proved ideal for the Ormsary service. It was also on occasions hired to MacBrayne's for the Lochgilphead to Ardrishaig local service. Advertised for sale in Setember 1965, it was relicensed when the bus operation of Stag Garage was taken over, and ran for another year.

MacDonald and MacLellan's service from Ormsary to Ardrishaig had historically been operated by a dedicated micro bus, and USP328 was replaced by another new purpose-built vehicle which also turned out to be unique. The Scottish Co-operative Wholesale Society, based in Rutherglen, had built up a substantial coaching business after the war, and had purchased Skye Transport in 1946, which was taken over by MacBrayne's in 1958. They also built a few bus bodies, principally for Glasgow Corporation Education Department, as well as on five new Albions for Skye Transport. There were also two Bedford OBs for Bankfoot Motors, with bodies built at the former premises of the bodybuilder Cadogan in Perth, which was also taken over in 1946. ASB578C was a solitary Austin FGK40 with a 15 seat body fitted with a mail compartment new in May 1965, and it operated the Ormsary service until withdrawn in 1982. Previously trading as Lorne Garage in Ardrishaig, MacDonald and MacLellan took over the control of the bus operation of Stag Garage of Lochgilphead in May 1966, but not the garage itself. Three buses were taken over, but all were withdrawn by the end of September, and replaced by two former RNAS 10 year old Bedford SBGs with Mulliner 36 seat bodies previously based at Lossiemouth. They were re-registered DSB496-7D and appeared in a new chocolate and cream livery replacing the traditional maroon and cream, with both Stag Garage and Lorne Garage in sign letters where a destination screen would have been placed.

The colours of Stag Garage were blue, red and grey, although it had various proprietors over the years. In addition to school contracts, it operated a service via Kilmartin to the small scenic village of Ford at the southern end of Loch Awe, originally continuing on to Craignish. It operated from Lochgilphead except Tuesday and Thursday at 9.30 and 1.50 and also 10.30 pm on a Saturday, with SB7337 the regular bus. It was also a petrol engine Morris Commercial, but with a rare Wadham 27 seat body new in 1948, which passed to MacDonald and MacLellan with two Maudslay Marathons. These were FUS992 (92) and GUS412 (49) new to MacBrayne's in 1948 and 1949 with Park Royal 35 seat "coach" bodies and sold direct to Stag Garage in January and October 1963 respectively. FUS992 had operated out of Kinlochleven since 1960 and GUS412 had been allocated to Ardrishaig for many years. This photograph of GUS412 was taken at Ford by my great friend the late Robert Grieves who was arguably Scotland's finest transport historian with over 40 books to his credit including the highly acclaimed "Wheels Around" series. As a photographer he could produce evocative pictures with a magic quality of their own. GUS412 was one of 28 similar vehicles new in 1948-49 for long distance services, although four had mail compartments, of which GUS 930 (seen on page 37) was one. Many of these required extensive rebuilding because rainwater was leaking through the saloon windows, and most had the work carried out by Bennett of Glasgow with a few by Greig in Inverness. There were various minor differences which indicated that GUS412 was one of the first to be so treated in 1958 and by Bennett, and like all but two retains its sliding door.

Former MacBrayne's buses were a popular choice for many smaller operators in the Highlands and Islands and rural parts of Scotland, and Argyll was no exception. One such operator was Malcolm McLachlan of Tayvallich who operated two such vehicles, both of which are now preserved back in MacBrayne's colours. The first was HGG359 (149), one of six Thornycroft Nippies (144-149) new in 1950 with 20 seat bodies built by Croft of Gallowgate, Glasgow purchased on 15th June 1962 for £150. The company had recondtioned and also built bus bodies throughout the war, continuing production until 1951. Croft bodies were also fitted to fifteen Commers and four Maudslays for MacBrayne's. Unusually none of the Thornycrofts were ever fitted with mail compartments, and spent most of their lives on the islands, with 144-147 latterly on Skye and 148 on South Uist, and were withdrawn in 1962 and 1963. HGG357 (147) was sold on 1st October 1962, also for £150, to nearby Archie McEachern of Kilberry who operated into Tarbert, and it ended up as a caravan near Lochgilphead. HGG359 when new was allocated to Inveraray for the mail service to Ardrishaig. Later on Islay, it was garaged at Port Charlotte as a spare bus for hires, funerals, church runs and duplication. Coincidentally it was succeeded there by Bedford OLAZ KGD904 (163) which Malcolm McLachlan also acquired. In 1961 HGG359 returned to the mainland as the spare bus at Lochgoilhead but was sold in June 1962.

Malcolm MacLachlan operated into Ardrishaig from his base at Tayvallich, via Bellanoch where the bus reversed and turned east along the Crinan Canal past Cairnbaan to join the A816 down to Lochgilphead. There was also a service from Achnamara, and in addition a mail service which commenced from the hamlet of Kilmory at the far end of Loch Sween heading north through Kilmichael to the secluded village of Achnamara. From there the route followed an unclassified road to Barnluasgan where a connection could be made with the service bus coming up the B8025 from Tayvallich. The photograph above was taken on 15th November 1968 at the road junction beside the North Knapdale War Memorial. HGG359 shown on the previous page is approaching the junction from Tayvallich, and in the photograph above is meeting Ford Transit HVM664F which has arrived from Kilmory. It had a 12 seat Martin Walker body, and was sold to MacDonald and MacLellan in November 1970 when it was replaced by Ford Transit MSB643J. Bedford OLAZ KGD904 had arrived in October 1967, and like KGD905-6 which had been at Lochgoilhead, had a 20 seat Duple body with a mail compartment. Both it and HGG359 operated the service at different times until the company was put up for sale in 1971. However, the service was not taken over by West Coast Motors until the following year. They were both sold for preservation and still appear in MacBrayne's colours at events, HGG359 being kept at the GVVT museum at Bridgeton, and KGD904 at Howmore in South Uist.

Eleven miles south of Ardrishaig is Tarbert where West Coast Motors had a small garage which it acquired in 1949 when it took over the business of Dickie Brothers of Tarbert, who had a garage, a taxi service and also operated lorries and buses. The garage and lorries were sold to Mundell of Tarbert and WCM took over the tours and bus operation. This expanded over the years, and Duple Vista bodied Bedford VAS CDC496C was photographed outside the depot on 22nd June 1979, waiting to leave for the Kilberry school service which WCM had acquired from McEachern in June 1967. There were also runs out to Kilberry at 9.00 and 2.30 on Tuesdays and Fridays. New to Beggs Coaches of Thornaby in 1965, it was actually purchased in April 1966 for a contract to meet the BEA flights arriving at the terminal in Campbeltown, and transport any passengers to the RAF base at Machrihanish. This service had previously been provided by Archie Malcolm, owner of The Royal Hotel in Campbeltown, with his Bedford OB. If the weather was inclement or the plane was not fit to fly, then it took passengers back to Glasgow. There were usually three other coaches kept there at that time, and an extra bus from Campbeltown on a Saturday night for duplication on a Sunday. The other service operated was out to Claonaig to meet the car ferry from Lochranza which started in December 1971 and similar Bedford VAS HXG307F, also bought from Beggs of Thornaby in 1968, or NSB303J were usually allocated. There was also normally a coach for private hires, and a spare vehicle which for many years was Duple Vega bodied Bedford SB ESB60 which like many of the fleet at the time was new to Gold Line of Dunoon.

The principal bus service which West Coast Motors obtained from Dickie Brothers was the "inter pier" service connecting East Loch Tarbert where the mail steamer *Loch Nevis* from Gourock called in, with West Loch Tarbert from which the boat departed for Islay. Sailing to Port Ellen or Port Askaig, it was met by two MacBrayne's mail buses, one for Portnahaven, and the other which was garaged on alternate nights at Port Ellen or Port Askaig. YYS174 operated the latter roster between May 1960 and May 1966. For many years, West Coast Motors used Bedford OBs on the connecting service between the piers, and on 4th May 1965, SB8280 was photographed at West Loch Tarbert with passengers for the 2.00 sailing on MV *Lochiel* to Port Ellen. It was the newest of seven OBs operated by West Coast, arriving in October 1950 and not withdrawn until 1969. It ended its days with West Coast Motors being kept in a corrugated-iron roofed shed beside Muasdale Inn for a school run to Tarbert. Also connecting with this boat was McConnachie's 11.30 service from Campbeltown and MacBrayne's 9.00 departure from Glasgow. In addition MacBrayne's mail bus from Ardrishaig arrived at 12.10, having collected any passengers arriving there off the coach from Oban. MacBrayne's always operated this service with a small bus, which was kept overnight in their single bus garage on Barn Brae in Inveraray for the 7.40 am departure to Ardrishaig. The regular bus from July 1963 when it was new until Western SMT took over was Bedford VAS 847HUS (94) which had a Duple Northern service bus body with 30 seats but surprisingly no mail compartment.

There had been competition on the service between Campbeltown and Tarbert which dated back to 1921, when the Royal Mail contract to meet the steamer at Tarbert was awarded to brothers Archie and Peter McConnachie who owned the Argyll Arms hotel and garage in Campbeltown. They purchased a bus and from that date built up a company which had between nine and eleven vehicles during the 1960s, but finally sold out to West Coast Motors on 28th February 1970. The Craig Brothers, who had set up business in 1919, started competing in 1922 using the fleetname West Coast Motor Service Company, and in 1925 started a morning service from Tarbert to Campbeltown, later extended to Lochgilphead. In 1930 West Coast Motors won the mail contract which they retained thereafter. It was then discovered that McConnachie's were not legally entitled to any of the licences, but an agreement was made that they could retain the 11.30 am return journey from Campbeltown. West Coast Motors operated the remainder of the service, and when this photograph was taken of SB8500 on 4th May 1965 on Harbour Street leaving Tarbert at 12.50, there were weekday departures from Campbeltown at 7.15, 9.45 and 1.00, returning from Tarbert at 9.05, 12.50 and 7.20. There were also school services from Muasdale and Tayinloan to Campbeltown, and a bus was kept overnight in a garage at Tayinloan which also provided a Saturday evening service at 5.15 to provide transport for those attending the cinema and other events in Campbeltown, returning at 10.30 pm.

West Coast Motors SB8500 was a Leyland Royal Tiger new in August 1952 with a 39 seat Burlingham Seagull body. It was their first underfloor engine vehicle, and was actually purchased for the service from Campbeltown to Southend. The route was pioneered by William McKerral of Southend and was sold to West Coast Motors in 1938. The only all week journeys to Southend at that time were at 7.45 and 4.00 from Campbeltown, and this allowed it to operate the 9.45 am departure to Tarbert. It was withdrawn early in 1970 and used to provide transport for mentally handicapped children. By comparison, McConnachie's PUJ782 in the photograph above, which was parked at Tarbert awaiting to depart at 2.30 on 16th November 1968, was a Leyland Royal Tiger with a Mark 5 41 seat Burlingham Seagull body and front entrance. This allowed it to be operated OMO, and it was fitted with a portable post box, and regularly operated the 11.30 service to Tarbert. In fact mail was carried on all West Coast Motors and McConnachie's services except on the Campbeltown local service. It was new to JT Whittle and Sons of Highley in January 1958, passing to Hall of Waterbeck in 1963, and arriving at Campbeltown in August 1964 via the dealer Millburn Motors in Glasgow. It passed to West Coast Motors in February 1970 when the business was sold, and was painted into their colours. It was then sold to MacDonald and MacLellan of Ardrishaig who retained the livery, and was finally withdrawn in 1977.

The main road between Tarbert and Campbeltown was down the A83 following the west coast of the Kintyre peninsula. There was, however, a service on the sparsely populated east side, from Campbeltown north to the fishing village of Carradale, and on Tuesdays and Fridays on the summer timetable a single run extended to Claonaig. During the war when the daily steamer service which called at Carradale was withdrawn, the service had run right through to Tarbert. Subsequently the through service was withdrawn but on a Friday the bus would travel light across from Claonaig to Tarbert, and either duplicate the 7.20 pm service back to Campbeltown or return over the weekend depending on operational requirements. On a Tuesday, the service would normally be operated by a Tarbert Depot coach going light down to Campbeltown to take up the 4.00 service to Carradale and Claonaig, and thus return light to Tarbert. Whether passengers were carried on the untimetabled section between Carradale and Tarbert I never found out, despite having a family holiday near Carradale in July 1973. The car ferry between Claonaig and Lochranza had started in December 1971, but this single journey from Campbeltown was unrelated, and there was already a rudimentary bus service between Tarbert and Claonaig. The service between Campbeltown and Carradale had been started by Jack Sommerville in 1928 but was sold to West Coast Motors in 1936. Because of the nature of the road with steep corners and few passing places, small vehicles were usually allocated with the driver having his own regular bus. While Bedfords had always been their bus of choice, West Coast Motors did buy a couple of unusual vehicles before reverting to Bedford SBs.

The most unusual bus to be purchased to operate the Campbeltown to Carradale service was PSB575K, seen on the previous page, which I photographed on Friday 20th July 1973. This was a day when the service continued beyond Carradale to Claonaig, and I followed it overtaking when possible, and took this photograph on a section of the route north of Carradale near Grogport with Arran in the background. The destination screen remained set for Carradale, but the few passengers on board would no doubt have been regular travellers. As it happens, I know the bus continued on to Tarbert, returning to Campbeltown that night. PSB575K was a Seddon with a 36 seat body built by Pennine Coachcraft new in July 1972, and bought for this service. It was replaced by an even less successful midibus in August 1976, and sold to Gray of Killin in 1977. The successor was MSB155R, a Bristol LHS6L with a Plaxton 35 seat coach body which was sold two years later to Sproat of Ulverston and ended up with a Welsh operator James Bros of Llangeitho. The service then reverted back to Bedford operation with a 7'6" wide SB5 model JSB445P with a 41 seat Duple Dominant body, replaced by similar USB180T. The service was operated from Campbeltown, but a school bus was kept at Carradale to take scholars down to Campbeltown. Operational flexibility was always required in a rural area with vehicles outstationed, and the picture above was taken on Tuesday 17th July 1973 when I drove to Claonaig and photographed GSB571 which had arrived on the 4.00 service from Campbeltown. A Bedford SB1 new in 1961 with a 41 seat Duple Super Vega body, it had been acquired from Gold Line of Dunoon seven years previously.

While West Coast Motors had services from Campbeltown to Carradale and Southend, McConnachie had always operated the local service, school runs, provided staff transport for the Kintyre Colliery at Machrihanish, and also operated the service there. Operating from a garage adjacent to the Argyll Arms Hotel which the company owned, there was much variety among the vehicles, particularly during the 1960s, and a leaning towards full size vehicles rather than lightweight Bedfords. This photograph of the interior of part of the depot was taken on 26th July 1965 when there were eleven active members of the fleet. In the corner delicensed is AEC Regal BCP534 an AEC Regal new in 12/49 to Halifax Corporation (345) with a Roe rear entrance body, upseated to 36. It was bought with BCP535 in 1959 to add capacity to the local services, and as the company had a policy of using conductresses on their services at that time, loading was easy and efficient. With the more powerful 9.6 litre engine it was well able to cope with the rural terrain. BCP535 was not withdrawn until 1967 and is now preserved at the West of England Transport Museum in Exeter. Parked beside it is Duple bodied SB8159 new to McConnachie in May 1950, and one of only two Bedford OBs operated by the company, despite the model being very popular for rural services. On the left is GWU570 a Leyland PS1 new to Ripponden and District in 1947 with a 33 seat Duple coach body with a manually operated door which passed to Hebble Motor Services in 1957 when the company was taken over. Used principally on school services, it was withdrawn in 1967 and sold to the contractor Rankin of Sandbank.

Purchased specifically for the Campbeltown local service in 1951 was Leyland Royal Tiger SB8250 with a rare Duple Roadmaster body which I photographed on 26th July 1965. This was a coach design, but was not successful and only 21 are believed to have been built. It uniquely was delivered as a service bus with 45 hard back seats but had a very narrow folding door at the front and was not universally popular. The PSU1/11 chassis designation indicated the 7'6" wide body which suited the narrow roads of southern Kintyre and with the large 9.8 litre engine, it was well-equipped to deal with the hills. While McConnachie used setright ticket machines on all the other services, as did West Coast Motors and MacBrayne's, the Campbeltown local service used the ultimate system, and SB8250 was later converted for OMO operation. It was McConnachie's first underfloor engined vehicle, and indeed the first to operate in Kintyre, and was locally known as the "prefab" because of its rather austere appearance. Out of use by 1968, it was sold to the builder Leech of Newcastle in 1970. In 1950 McConnachie had been granted a licence to operate a local service to serve the post-war housing estates which had been built and there was a regular service throughout the day connecting Meadows and Calton with the High Street from 7.45 am to 7.12 pm and later runs at 8.30 and 10.40.

The first double decker to operate in Kintyre arrived in 1961, having travelled the 600 miles up from Devon with ease. Its role was to operate the Campbeltown to Machranish service which had been in McConnachie's hands since 1933 when the Machrihanish and Campbeltown Light Railway who were awarded the contract three years previously had gone into liquidation. KOD 585 was new to Devon General (DR585) in August 1949 as one of a batch of 26 AEC Regents with Weymann 56 seat bodies. As model 9621E, it was 7'6" feet wide, and had the same powerful 9.6 litre engine as BCP534 and 535, a Wilson preselector gearbox and at the shorter length of 26 feet was an ideal vehicle for this service. It created a great deal excitement when it arrived, and proved very popular with locals and tourists alike. It was withdrawn in late 1966, and sold for preservation to the West of England Transport Museum in Exeter in March 1967 returning on the long journey down south to join BCP535. Repainted back into Devon General colours, it is a popular attendee at rallies. There were eight departures to Machrihanish on weekdays and ten on a Saturday, the first being at 8.05 in the morning and the last at 10 pm. The requirement for a double decker was reinforced when a large number of tourists descended from the turbine excursion steamers, the *Duchess of Hamilton* and the *Duchess of Montrose* for a tour to "The Shores of the Atlantic."

There was even more excitement when two former 15 year old London Transport double deckers arrived in June 1966, acquired from the dealer Passenger Vehicle Sales of Upminster, KYY812 former RTL842 and LLU907 former RTL917. They were both Leyland Titan PD2s with Metro-Cammell bodies and both entered service in October 1950. Again they had powerful engines, the same 9.8 litre engine as SB8250, and were also only 7'6" wide and like KOD585 very suitable for the work they had to do. Both KYY812 and LLU907 had the usual four yearly body overhaul required by London Transport, and retained their original bodies on the first occasion, but as was customary received a different body at the next two overhauls. Both remained in service until a month before their sale in May 1966. They subsequently passed to West Coast Motors with the sale of the business on 28th February 1970 but were not used and were sold to Telefilms Transport of Preston in May. High capacity single deckers replaced them, and with the doubling of the bus grant in November 1971, so that 50% of the cost of a new vehicle could be subsidised provided it was used on stage carriage services for half of the time in the first five years, there was an imperative to purchase new buses. In April 1974 the highest capacity single decker in Scotland arrived in Campbeltown VSB164M, a Bedford YRT with a 60 seat Plaxton Derwent body. KYY812 was photographed at the bus office in Main Street on 14th November 1968 waiting to depart on the 10.50 pm local service. Unlike KOD585 no destination screen was fitted, and slip-boards in the front passenger window were used instead.

Back up in Tarbert, despite the destination "Campbeltown," Western SMT Bristol RELH6G DSD704D (MT2063) sits on the pier waiting to take the return journey back to Glasgow at 2.30 on 14th July 1973. It was one of 21 luxurious, toilet equipped 38 seat Alexander bodied London coaches new in 1966 which were replaced by Bristol REMHs with Alexander M type bodies. Eleven of these subsequently operated out of Thornliebank Depot between 1972 and 1976 until Alexander T type bodied Seddons MSJ376-80P (MS2570-4) came. However, there were never more than six at any one time, with four usually based at Ardrishaig, the regulars being DSD703-5/10D. At Thornliebank they were confined to this service, having been introduced to upgrade the specification of coach employed. The vehicle outstationed at Inveraray was by now a full size bus, and DSD705D became the regular allocation. The entire batch had been converted to have 45 non reclining seats without toilets, and their one piece doors altered to air operation for OMO work. The seating capacity was limited to 45 as an increase would have required an additional rear emergency door on the nearside due to a change in the law. With the exception of this bus, the entire batch ended up in Dumfries and Galloway in cream and red dual purpose livery, and were all withdrawn by 1980. DSD704D was not so fortunate. It was new at Kilmarnock Depot on 1st March 1966 for the London service and transferred to Johnstone in September 1969 for duplication on the Lancashire services. It was delicensed for conversion in February 1972, and re-entered service in April 1973 but it was burnt out in March 1974. Its remains were finally disposed of to Cunningham of Elderslie two years later after a decision was made not to re-body it.

Waiting at Ardrishaig bus stance on the same day is Highland Omnibuses Alexander bodied AEC Reliance RMS738 (B79) due to return to Oban at 1.15. The corresponding Western SMT vehicle from Ardrishaig was unusually an Alexander bodied Bristol MW6G OCS722 (MT1600), deputising for Bedford VAS EGA834C (E3), such was the variety of buses now operating in the former MacBrayne's territory. When the MacBrayne's empire was broken up and the Ardrishaig area services passed to Western SMT, Highland Omnibuses assumed control of the Alexander Midland operation in Oban in October 1970. Nine of the fourteen vehicles were Leyland Tiger Cubs, non standard for the Highland fleet, and were exchanged with three somewhat older AEC Monocoaches and six Reliances given fleet numbers B72-7/9-81 (78 was already on Midland's Oban allocation.) Initially, the Ardrishaig service was operated by Highland B76 in Midland livery from Oban, and Western were lent Bedford VAS 847HUS (which had been the regular bus at Inveraray) now Highland CD76 still in MacBrayne's colours, to operate the Ardrishaig end, with identical E3 in black and white livery deputising! RMS738 had been new as Alexander Midland MAC204 at Stepps Depot in April 1961. It was later reallocated north from Oban Depot to Dingwall in 1974 where it languished on local work, ended up in the "pool" by 1976, and was sold for scrap in 1977. Parked beside it is McLachlan's ex MacBrayne's KGD904 waiting to return to Tayvallich.

The MacBrayne's buses between Kinlochleven and Fort William called in at Corran Ferry to collect any passengers, including those from the connecting bus services arriving from Acharacle and Kilchoan, and a bus with a mail compartment was garaged at each location overnight. Ardgour and Acharacle Motor Services had gone into liquidation on 31st December 1950, and MacBrayne's had taken over the services but not their two mail buses. A bus left Kilchoan at 7 am for Acharacle, connecting with the bus from Acharacle at Salen which proceeded to Corran Ferry arriving at 10.15. On a Saturday the Acharacle bus started from Kinlochmoidart, and on a Monday there was an additional run from Acharacle at 6.30 am for the pupils who were staying in the hostels during the week. Maudslay Marathon FGB418 (35) was photographed on 3rd September 1964 leaving the ferry on the 10.00 service from Kinlochleven to Fort William. It and FGA159 (15) were the first Maudslays to be purchased after the war when new bodies were in short supply, and were fitted with second hand Park Royal bodies from Maudslay Meteors which were new in 1929 and themselves re-bodied in 1936, with the body fitted to FGB418 coming from SB3362. The pair were later re-bodied in 1958 with Duple bodies similar to that on KGG709 seen on page 55, and FGB418 spent most of its subsequent life based at Fort William depot. It was withdrawn in December 1967 and sold to Garner of Bridge of Weir. In the corner of the picture is a former Dodds of Troon Guy Arab DTY789 with a rare Gurney Nutting body rebuilt with a full front.

Back cover: Descending to Corran Ferry in August 1962 is one of the quintessentially MacBrayne's coaches with a style of Park Royal body favoured by the company for over ten years. Maudslay Marathon FUS997 (97) had only two more months left in service, but was not sold until March 1963 when it was bought by Smith of Grantown for £140, and spent the next two years transporting skiers in the Cairngorms. Unlike GUS412 seen on page 9, it was never rebuilt and was the last Maudslay to be sold with side windows which retained their original ornate design. Kept overnight at North Ballachulish, it was operating the 10.25 service from there to Fort William.

The Buses of Arran, Argyll and environs

in colour photographs by John Sinclair

£12.95

ISBN 978 1 84033 834 8

Published by:
Stenlake Publishing Limited
54–58 Mill Square, Catrine,
Ayrshire, KA5 6RD.
01290 551122
www.stenlake.co.uk

Facing page: Oban continued to be a colourful place under Highland control, and even after the former MacBrayne's and Midland vehicles had been joined by others from Highland Omnibuses own fleet there was continuing variety, as a new livery of peacock blue and poppy red was introduced for service buses to recall the now extinct MacBrayne's colours. Highland Omnibuses own coach livery of blue and grey also provided contrasting colours. The initial Highland Omnibuses Oban allocation in October 1970 consisted of sixteen vehicles, with eleven AECs (two Monocoaches and five Reliances from Alexander Midland and four Reliances from MacBrayne's), two Albion Vikings, one Bristol LH (SWG678H) one 36' Leyland Leopard and one Bedford VAS. As always there were continual exchanges and non standard SWG678H was transferred to Eastern Scottish and replaced by XGD775. It came from the original MacBrayne's Fort William service bus fleet and was new in August 1959 as an AEC Reliance with a 45 seat Park Royal-Roe body to BET design, and with XGD776 (numbered 41-2) operated Fort William local services until taken over by Highland in May 1970 and renumbered B44-5. XGD776 remained at Fort William and was delicensed in September 1975 and sold for scrap. XGD775 was photographed on 19th August 1972 with McCaig's Tower in the background, heading for Ganavan Sands at 10.05 having arrived in from Bonawe where it was the regular "sleeper." It was transferred north to Aviemore in 1973, also delicensed in 1975 and sold in May 1976 to Sutherland of Glenbrittle on Skye, who ran it for the next three years.

North of Oban is Connel Bridge which spans Loch Etive at its narrowest point and is a category B listed structure. It was constructed for the railway branch line between Connel Ferry Station and Ballachulish which opened in 1903 and provided a link between the slate quarries at Ballachulish and the Oban to Glasgow freight trains. In 1914 a roadway was added to the bridge, but road traffic and trains were not permitted on the bridge at the same time. In March 1966 the railway line was finally closed, and the road was converted for the exclusive use of road vehicles and pedestrians. In August, when this photograph was taken, the railway track had not yet been lifted, and only 7'6" wide buses were permitted to cross. MacBrayne's used the occasion to introduce a through service from Kinlochleven to Oban with three journeys each way on weekdays and four on a Saturday, and KGG709 is operating the 3.20 departure from Kinlochleven, a journey timetabled to take all of two hours and 20 minutes. One of three AEC Regals KGG708-10 (12/27/30) new in 1952 with 35 seat Roe service bus bodies, and the last half cab vehicles to enter the MacBrayne's fleet, it and KGG708 were fitted with new 7'6" wide Duple coach bodies in 1961. This was an attempt to modernise the appearance of some of the older vehicles which were still used on long distance services, and four Maudslays were similarly re-bodied. In practice KGG708-10 all operated this service with KGG710 on the morning school run from Ballachulish to Oban, but once the track had been lifted, eight feet wide AEC Reliances with Duple Midland bodies were used and UGB428 (178) Macbrayne's first member of this class was a regular. KGG709 was withdrawn in 1970 and sold to a contractor in Barrhead.

Although Kinlochleven was now linked to Oban, Fort William and Glasgow by direct services, there was also a local bus service to Ballachulish Ferry as the Ballachulish bridge was not opened until December 1975. There were also two runs through Glencoe to Crianlarich Station to connect with the trains from Glasgow to Fort William, and I photographed HGA980D on 27th August 1971 at Glencoe Crossroads on the 8.10 service from Crianlarich Station to Kinlochleven. It had left the depot at 6.15 am to arrive at the railway station at 7.55 and collect mail and any passengers off the 5.50 train from Glasgow to Fort William. It then returned with the mail, doubling back to Ballachulish, and then along the north banks of Loch Leven to terminate back at the Depot. The afternoon service left Fort William at 3.00 returning from Crianlarich at 7.15, or 8.40 on a Friday when there was a late train, and was operated by Fort William Depot with a full size bus. HGA980D was one of ten Beford VAS HGA976-985D (203-212) new in 1966 with Willowbrook bodies. HGA980-984D had mail compartments with only 24 rather than 28 seats, and were scattered throughout the MacBrayne's empire all allocated to specific routes where this was a requirement. As a mail service, this journey always required a bus with a mail compartment and 14 seat Bedford OLAZ KGE242 (170) was the regular for many years. HGA980D arrived new to Kinlochleven and in fact operated this particular journey right through to January 1976 when the depot was closed whereupon it was withdrawn and passed via the dealer Ensign of Benfleet to Beard Coaches of Widecombe in Devon. It was already owned by Highland Omnibuses when photographed carrying fleet number CD68, but was not painted into their colours of peacock blue and poppy red until July 1972.

The Country Houses and Castles of Royal Deeside

Volume One: Lower Deeside

W. Stewart Wilson

Front cover: Birse Castle.